WYATT EARP

LEGENDS OF THE WEST

WYATT EARP

Published by Creative Education, 123 South Broad Street, Mankato, Minnesota 56001
Creative Education is an imprint of The Creative Company
Design and Production by EvansDay Design

Photographs by Arizona Historical Society/Tucson (27242, 30225, 30226, 14835, 12169, 29872),
Buffalo Bill Historical Center; Cody, Wyoming; Vincent Mercaldo Collection (P.71.2062.1, front,
p. 2; P.71.2067, p. 15), Corbis (Bettmann, Bureau L.A. Collection, Michael Freeman, John Springer
Collection, Minnesota Historical Society, John McAnulty, David Muench, Charles O'Rear,
Gabe Palmer, ML Sinibaldi), Kansas State Historical Society

Library of Congress Cataloging-in-Publication Data
Goodman, Michael E. Wyatt Earp / by Michael E. Goodman.
p. cm. — (Legends of the West)
ISBN 1-58341-339-1

1. Earp, Wyatt, 1848-1929—Juvenile literature. 2. Peace officers—Southwest,
New—Biography—Juvenile literature. 3. United States marshals—Southwest,
New—Biography—Juvenile literature. 4. Southwest, New—Biography—
Juvenile literature. 5. Tombstone (Ariz.)—History—19th century—Juvenile
literature. I. Title. II. Legends of the West (Mankato, Minn.)
F786.E18G66 2005   978'.02'092—dc22   2004056165

First edition

2 4 6 8 9 7 5 3 1

Cover and page 2 photograph:
Wyatt Earp—and his famous handlebar mustache—in his formative years

⊷⊶ **Michael E. Goodman** ⊷⊶

BAT MASTERSON, ONE OF THE MOST COLORFUL LAWMEN AND GAMBLERS OF THE OLD WEST,

once wrote that the Western frontier "knew no braver or [more] desperate man than Wyatt Earp."

Wyatt risked his life maintaining order in some of the most lawless towns in the Old West—places such as Dodge City and Tombstone, where drunken cowboys and ruthless bandits rode through the streets or fought nightly in saloons and gambling halls.

He was a crack shot, though he preferred to use his long-barrel gun as a club to knock out lawbreakers rather than kill them. Yet he became famous for the two times he did shoot to kill—during a wild 30-second gunfight in Tombstone, and during a murderous rampage to avenge his brother's killing a few months later.

Wyatt Earp was part hero, part outlaw, part gambler, part businessman, part outsider, and part family man. His fame was born in the 1880s, but it grew even greater in the 1930s and 1950s, when his story began to be told and retold in books, movies, and television shows. And with each retelling, more facts and more exaggeration were added, until it became difficult to separate the man from the legend. Today, Wyatt Earp remains a symbol of the courage and foolhardiness it took to survive in the Old West.

A Natural Leader

WYATT WAS BORN ON MARCH 19, 1848, IN

MONMOUTH, ILLINOIS,

AND NAMED FOR HIS FATHER'S ARMY COMMANDER

in the Mexican War,

CAPTAIN WYATT BERRY STAPP.

Even though Wyatt was the fourth son in the Earp family, he was

always the leader among his brothers and sisters. His parents,

Virginia and Nicholas, had met and married in Kentucky and

later moved to Illinois. Virginia Cooksey Earp was descended

from an English family that had settled in eastern Virginia in

the early 1700s and moved across the Appalachians after 1800.

Nicholas Earp was of Scotch descent. He was a trained lawyer, though what he really wanted to do was farm his own land. So, in 1850, Nicholas moved the family to Pella, Iowa. They lived in Pella and planted corn on an 80-acre (32 ha) spread just outside town. Over time, the family grew to include seven children. They were a close-knit group, and Wyatt developed particularly strong bonds with his older brother Virgil and younger brother Morgan.

When Wyatt was 13, the Civil War broke out. His three older brothers enlisted in the Union Army, while Wyatt had to stay home and take charge of the corn crop. Always hard-working, Wyatt carried out his responsibilities well but dreamed of being a fighter instead of a farmer. The next spring, Wyatt—now tall, blonde, blue-eyed, and looking much older than 14—tried to sneak away to enlist. His father caught him before he could reach the recruitment office, however, and made him come back home. Wyatt continued doing his farm chores diligently, but he spent his free time practicing his marksmanship with one of his father's old army guns.

In 1864, the Earp boys returned from the war, and the family joined a wagon train heading to California. Nicholas was one of the leaders of the wagon train, and Wyatt, now 16, had an important job, too. Using a combination rifle and shotgun his father had given him, Wyatt hunted animals to feed the travelers and helped protect the wagon train from attacks by hostile Indians.

The Earps settled near San Bernardino, California. Wyatt split his time between helping on the family ranch and working on a stagecoach line delivering mail and freight. Driving the stage was

Nicholas and Virginia Cooksey Earp produced seven children, including Wyatt, who became one of the West's most famous lawmen.

Bat Masterson

As many Western legends have been told about Bat Masterson as about Wyatt Earp. Born William Barclay Masterson in Illinois, he came to the West as a teenager. He was said to have had his first gunfight in Texas in 1876 in a fight over a woman. He was shot in the leg and needed a cane to help him walk for the rest of his life. Some say his nickname, "Bat," was short for Barclay. Others say he got the nickname because he would use his cane as a bat to club outlaws over the head. The lives of Wyatt Earp and Bat Masterson were closely intertwined. The two men met while hunting buffalo in Wyoming in the late 1860s. In 1876, they served together as deputies in Dodge City. Later, Bat provided Wyatt, Doc Holliday, and Wyatt's brother Warren asylum in Colorado after the "vendetta ride." During his life, Masterson was an outstanding lawman, a successful gambler, and a respected sportswriter and promoter.

a difficult job because of the roughness of the terrain, the poor quality of horses the stagecoach owner had bought, and the possibility of attacks by bandits. Legend has it that when the regular driver broke his leg, the boss asked the driver to recommend a replacement. "Get Nicholas Earp's boy, Wyatt," he was told. "You've got bad horses and bad men to handle on that run, and young Wyatt Earp can do both."

When the driver was ready to come back to work, Wyatt and his older brother Virgil began working for another stage line that operated between southern California and western Arizona. It was a hard way for a teenage boy to make a living, but Wyatt enjoyed the excitement.

Another family move cut short Wyatt's stay in California. Nicholas Earp missed his mother and brothers, who had remained in the Midwest. He took his wife and children back eastward by train, finally settling in Lamar, Missouri; however, Wyatt and Virgil decided to leave the train in Wyoming to seek adventure. Wyatt took on two very different jobs: hunting game to feed the men building the rail lines, and either refereeing or handling bets on boxing matches. For much of the rest of his life, Wyatt was interested in boxing. He never fought in any prize fights himself, but he often used his fists instead of his gun to knock down men who broke the law.

In 1868, 20-year-old Wyatt joined his family in Lamar, intending to settle down there. By now, he was more than six feet (1.8 m) tall and had begun sporting a mustache. He was thin but strong and

This photograph depicts a live cattle auction in the late 1800s. Wyatt got his start as a lawman in booming Kansas "cow towns."

walked with an upright stride. Wyatt worked in a hotel and soon married the owner's teenage daughter, Urilla. He also ran for the position of town constable, defeating his half-brother Newton in a close race. It was Wyatt's first law enforcement job. At the time, lawmen were paid part of their salary based on the number of arrests they made, and since Lamar was a quiet town with little crime, Constable Earp didn't earn much money.

Wyatt's life changed dramatically less than a year later, when Urilla died suddenly of typhoid fever. He was devastated by her death and later got into some trouble in town when he was accused of overcharging a Lamar man for police services. Unable to cope with the stress of trying to prove his innocence, Wyatt stole a horse and fled to Arkansas. For the first time in his life, Wyatt was an outlaw.

Eventually the charges against him were dropped, but Wyatt never returned to Lamar. Instead, he headed to the Indian Territories (now Oklahoma), where he made a living hunting and skinning buffalo. Wyatt developed lasting friendships with several of his fellow buffalo hunters, including two future legendary lawmen, Bat Masterson and Bill Tilghman. He also earned a reputation among the hunters for being hardworking, sober, even-tempered, and (in Bat Masterson's words) "absolutely destitute of physical fear."

But Wyatt had good business sense as well as courage. He saw that there was not much economic future in hunting buffalo. Instead, the cattle business was becoming the West's most important industry. Prosperous towns were springing up along rail lines in Kansas. Cowboys from Texas drove herds of cattle to towns such as Ellsworth, Wichita, and Dodge City, where the cattle could be shipped to feed hungry people in the East. After weeks on the trail, the cowboys were restless and looking for fun. They had money to spend on drinking, gambling, and women, and they had guns to shoot up the towns.

Kansas was just the place for a fearless young man who wanted to make money and who wasn't afraid to take a job enforcing the law. And Wyatt was well suited to be a Western lawman. He was tall and strong; he was an expert at handling horses and guns, and was good with his fists; he wasn't afraid to stand face-to-face with any man, even if the man was armed. He also had great respect for the law, something his father had taught him. And Wyatt had one other skill that proved invaluable—he developed loyal friendships. Friends such as Bat Masterson were willing to back him up during the most desperate times. Because he had the support of his friends and brothers, Wyatt would seldom find himself facing danger alone.

The records are not clear, but sometime in either 1873 or 1874, Wyatt Earp rode into Kansas, and his legend began.

Frontier Marshal

While writer Stuart Lake and television writers gave Wyatt the title of marshal, he never really earned that designation. Throughout his nine-year law enforcement career, Wyatt was always a deputy. He supposedly turned down a sheriff's job in Ellsworth, Kansas, after the showdown with Ben Thompson. In Dodge, he was in charge of the police force, but he held the title of assistant city marshal. In Tombstone, Wyatt was a deputy U.S. marshal, and his brother Virgil out-ranked him. Wyatt then failed to get the appointment he hoped for as town sheriff. Politics played a big part in the territorial governor's decision to appoint Democrat John Behan instead of Wyatt, who was a Republican. While he may never have held the top title, Wyatt was always recognized as a leader, especially in his own family. Even his older brothers Virgil and James usually followed his direction.

CHAPTER TWO

Finding Fame, Not Fortune

WYATT MOVED FROM TOWN TO TOWN IN KANSAS,
SERVING AS A LAWMAN
AND SUPPLEMENTING HIS INCOME BY
buying part interests in
SALOONS AND GAMBLING HALLS.

As a town deputy, Wyatt received a steady paycheck and a fee for every arrest he made. But arresting drunken cowboys could be a pretty dangerous way to make a living.

According to legend, Wyatt actually turned down the first sheriff's job he was offered. The incident occurred in Ellsworth in 1873. A cowboy named Billy Thompson got drunk and accidentally shot and killed the local sheriff. Billy's brother Ben drew his gun and threatened to kill anyone who stopped his brother from leaving town. No one except Wyatt was willing to confront Ben Thompson, so the mayor instantly appointed Wyatt a deputy marshal.

Bat Masterson lived the dangerous life of a lawman of the West before spending his last years as a sports journalist in New York.

Wyatt walked right up to Thompson and demanded that he lay down his gun and agree to be arrested. Thompson looked into Wyatt's hard eyes and gave up. In the end, the town judge, not wanting to anger the cowboys who spent so much money in Ellsworth, fined Thompson just $25 for disturbing the peace. When the mayor offered Wyatt the vacant sheriff's position at the high salary of $125 a month (the equivalent of almost $2,000 today), Wyatt declined. He said he didn't want to serve in a town where a sheriff's life was valued at only $25.

From Ellsworth, Wyatt moved to Wichita and was welcomed onto the police force. He quickly earned a reputation for hard work and honesty. However, after getting into a fight with his boss, Wyatt lost his job. So he headed to Texas to become a bounty hunter, chasing down thieves for the Wells Fargo Company. There, Wyatt met John "Doc" Holliday, a part-time dentist and full-time gambler and gunfighter. Holliday would become one of Wyatt's closest friends, risking his own life several times to back up Wyatt.

In 1876, Wyatt, now 28, headed to Dodge City, Kansas, the state's newest boomtown: Dodge City boasted 19 establishments licensed to sell liquor. The streets were dusty, and the smell of slaughtered meat and tanned hides hung in the air. Dodge City mayor George Hoover put Wyatt in charge of the police force, and Wyatt hired his brother Morgan and Bat Masterson, his old friend from Oklahoma, to help him tame the town.

While everyone on Wyatt's police force carried guns, they seldom fired them. More often, they subdued an outlaw by knocking him over the head with a gun barrel and leading him to jail. Wyatt and Bat called

Josephine Marcus Earp

Though she never fired a shot, Josie Marcus may have played a key role in the events that led up to the "Gunfight at the O.K. Corral." Josie (who was sometimes called "Sadie") grew up in a religious Jewish family in San Francisco. When she was 18 or 19, she ran away with an acting troupe that traveled to Arizona. There, a young lawman named John Behan met her and fell in love. The two became engaged, and Josie moved to Tombstone to be near her fiancé. Then Behan introduced her to Wyatt Earp, and she and Wyatt began an affair. Behan already had his differences with Wyatt, but losing Josie to his rival infuriated him. Behan may have added to the bad blood between the Earps and the Clantons that led up to the deadly gunfight, and he was quick to arrest Wyatt for murder afterwards. Wyatt and Josie were married in 1883 in San Francisco. The couple moved around together, prospecting, investing, and gambling for more than 45 years. They never had any children.

this method "buffaloing" because they had learned it while hunting buffalo. Wyatt said, "Mayor Hoover hired me to cut down on the killings in Dodge, not increase them."

Wyatt claimed that he killed only one man during his three years in Dodge—a cowboy who was shooting up the town at three o'clock one morning. But he did get involved in a number of showdowns. During one confrontation, Doc Holliday, who had recently moved to Dodge, shot and killed a man who was set to shoot Wyatt in the back. The incident proved once again how important friends could be to a Western lawman. Doc would join Wyatt in another dangerous gunfight several years later, and both men would etch their names forever in the history of the Wild West.

The fateful event took place in Tombstone, Arizona, on October 26, 1881. Two years earlier, Wyatt had left Dodge City and headed west to join his brothers Virgil and Morgan in Tombstone, where silver had been discovered. Doc Holliday moved there, too. Virgil became county sheriff, and Wyatt was hired as deputy U.S. marshal and tax collector of Pima County, near Tombstone. Wyatt hoped to become town sheriff, but the territory governor appointed John Behan instead.

Wyatt and Behan didn't get along. They disagreed politically: Wyatt was a Republican, and Behan was a Democrat. They disagreed about law enforcement: Wyatt distrusted Behan and thought he was connected to a local gang of outlaws and cowboys led by the Clanton family. They disagreed socially: Both of them were romantically involved with the same woman—a young actress from San Francisco named Josephine ("Josie") Marcus. Josie had been engaged to Behan but decided to leave him for Wyatt. Wyatt, in turn, deserted his common-law wife, Mattie Blaylock, whom he'd met in Dodge City, to start a relationship with Josie. (Wyatt and Josie would eventually marry and spend nearly 50 years together.)

Trouble between the Earps and the Clantons began brewing in Tombstone months before October 1881. Wyatt had aggressively investigated a stagecoach robbery and an incident of cattle rustling that involved members of the Clanton gang. The Clantons threatened to get Wyatt.

By the evening of October 25, the bad feelings were ready to boil over. That night, Ike Clanton and Tom McLaury got drunk and began calling for a showdown with the Earps. The next morning, both men were still making threats, and each was "buffaloed" by either Virgil or Wyatt. Gang members Billy Clanton, Frank McLaury, and Billy Claiborne soon joined Ike and Tom in town. The five men armed themselves and gathered by an open lot not far from the O.K. Corral.

Soon, the three Earp brothers, joined by Doc Holliday, came striding down the street toward the cowboys. All four men were dressed in black; the Earps were wearing handguns, and Doc carried a shotgun beneath his long coat. Sheriff Behan tried to stop them, saying he would disarm the cowboys, but they pushed right by him.

Just what happened next has been portrayed in different ways in many stories and movies. According to eyewitnesses and Wyatt's own testimony later, here is what occurred: Virgil, as marshal, called on the Clanton group to give up their guns; one cowboy might have cocked his weapon in response; then Wyatt and Frank McLaury be-

Tombstone, Arizona, sprang up in 1877 as a silver-mining town and hosted the infamous "Gunfight at the O.K. Corral" in 1881.

gan firing at almost the same time. Less than 30 seconds later, three of the cowboys lay dead, and Virgil, Morgan, and Doc were all bleeding from wounds. Wyatt was unhurt.

Behan immediately arrested the Earps and Doc Holliday for murder. The gunfight and the trial that followed received coverage in newspapers around the country. In the end, the judge decided that while the lawmen had acted "incautiously and without due circumspection" in engaging in the gunfight, he could "attach no criminality to their unwise act." He dismissed the case. Half of Tombstone applauded the verdict, while the other half still cried "Murder."

The trouble wasn't over, however. A few months later, Virgil was ambushed in the street in Tombstone and shot in his thigh and left arm. He was never able to regain full use of the arm and walked with a limp the rest of his life. In March 1882, several Clanton gang members opened fire on Wyatt and Morgan in a Tombstone pool hall. Wyatt escaped unharmed again, but Morgan died in his arms.

Wyatt vowed to avenge the attacks on his brothers, and so began his "vendetta ride." Over the next two weeks, Wyatt, with his brother Warren and Doc Holliday, tracked down the men suspected of shooting Morgan and mercilessly killed them all. When the vendetta was complete, the three men couldn't return to Tombstone; warrants for their arrest awaited them there. So they rode to Trinidad, Colorado, where Bat Masterson was city marshal. Bat convinced the Colorado governor not to turn in his friends, arguing that going back to Arizona would mean certain death. For Wyatt, it was a sad ending to his career as a Western lawman.

The "Buntline Special"

Wyatt Earp supposedly carried a unique six-shooter with an extra-long 12-inch (30.5 cm) barrel that Western writer Ned Buntline had given him as a token of appreciation after a visit to Dodge City. Writer Stuart Lake described this "Buntline special" in his book, and it was the weapon that television's Wyatt Earp used to tame outlaws in Dodge City in a 1950s series. After the series aired, children throughout the country halted imaginary bad guys with their own toy Buntline specials. But there is no evidence that the gun ever existed. Buntline claimed he had ordered five such weapons to be made by the Colt factory, yet there are no records of the guns ever being shipped, nor has any gun collector ever been able to obtain a surviving model. There is even doubt that Buntline ever visited Dodge City in the first place. It is more likely that Wyatt carried a Colt revolver with an eight-inch (20.3 cm) barrel—longer than the average gun, but not really "special."

CHAPTER THREE

Wyatt and Josie: Western Nomads

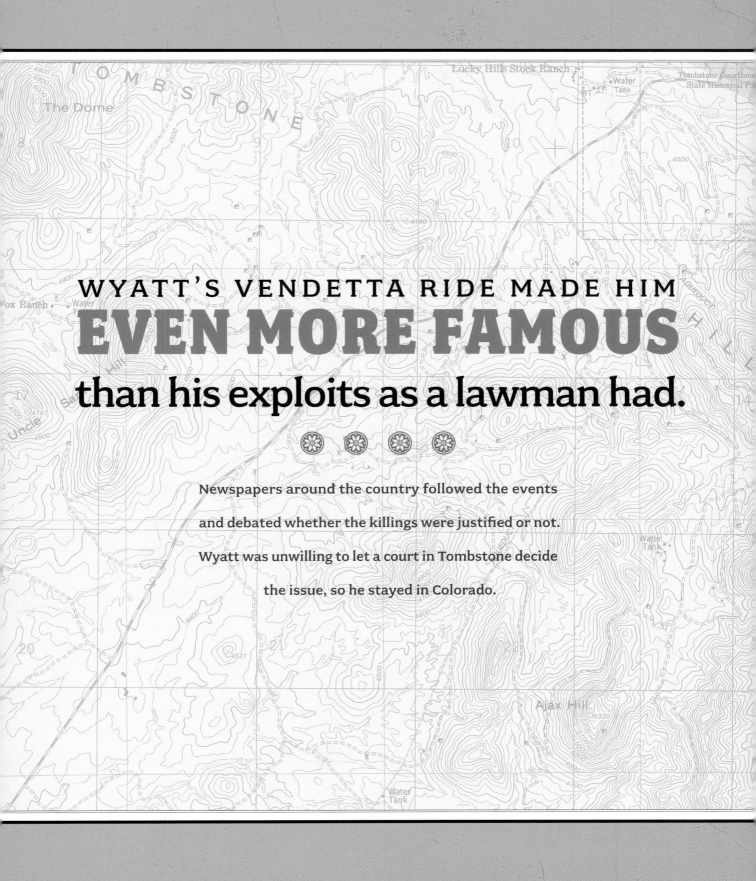

WYATT'S VENDETTA RIDE MADE HIM
EVEN MORE FAMOUS
than his exploits as a lawman had.

❀ ❀ ❀ ❀

Newspapers around the country followed the events

and debated whether the killings were justified or not.

Wyatt was unwilling to let a court in Tombstone decide

the issue, so he stayed in Colorado.

When Wyatt and Warren started on their vendetta, the rest of the Earps also left Tombstone for the family ranch in California, forfeiting all the property they had acquired in Arizona. Wyatt now found himself almost broke. He put his gambling skills to work in Colorado and managed to win nearly $10,000 at the gaming tables. Then he moved on to San Francisco and was joined by his brothers Virgil and Warren and their families. Wyatt reunited with Josie there and later married her.

For the next 20 years, Wyatt and Josie led a nomadic existence, continuing to seek their fortune. First, they headed back to Colorado, where Wyatt opened his own casino. Several times, he had to face down gamblers who accused the house of cheating them and threatened violence. Wyatt used a mixture of diplomacy and intimidation to defuse any problems and somehow avoided getting involved in any more shootouts.

Then, early in 1884, word came that gold had been found near Eagle City, Idaho. The Idaho gold rush was short-lived, but Wyatt once again made money in the saloon business. He also filed his own mining claims, though none of them yielded much gold. Wyatt and his brother James did make news in Idaho, however, when they rushed in to stop a gunfight between two groups battling over a land claim. The next day, the local newspaper reported: "With characteristic coolness, they stood where the bullets from both parties flew about them, joked with the participants about their poor marksmanship, and although they pronounced the affair a fine picture, used their best endeavors to stop the shooting."

Wyatt (left, on a beach in Alaska with former Tombstone mayor John P. Clum) spent time in Alaska during the region's gold rush.

Doc Holliday

J ohn Henry Holliday was born in Georgia in 1851. He moved to Philadelphia and trained to be a dentist, earning him the nickname "Doc." Holliday suffered from tuberculosis and often went into coughing fits. He was also a heavy drinker. Doc went west in the early 1870s, hoping the warm, dry air would improve his health. In Texas, Doc gained a reputation for his skill with a gun and for having a very bad temper. He often picked fights with other men and then shot them in "self-defense." Wyatt Earp and Doc first became friends in Texas around 1875. Doc later joined Wyatt in Dodge City and Tombstone, and took part in the Gunfight at the O.K. Corral and the "vendetta ride." Doc was always loyal to Wyatt, possibly because Wyatt never shunned him because of his tuberculosis. Doc died in a Colorado hospital in 1887. His last words, "It's funny–," may have been a comment on how funny it was that he was dying in bed rather than in a gunfight.

When the Idaho gold rush was over, Wyatt and Josie headed south, planning to settle in San Diego, California. Along the way, they stopped in Denver, where an old friend, Doc Holliday, greeted them. Doc, who had long suffered from tuberculosis, was clearly dying. "Isn't it strange," Wyatt said, "that if it were not for you, I wouldn't be alive today, yet you must go first." Doc died in November 1887 at the age of 36.

Wyatt and Josie spent two years in San Diego, investing in real estate and race horses, before returning to San Francisco. The couple led a quiet life for the next several years, with Wyatt making news only once, in 1896, when he was asked to referee a national championship boxing match between Tom Sharkey and Bob Fitzsimmons. The match was being fought under new rules, one of which called for disqualification for hitting below the belt. More than 10,000 spectators packed San Francisco's Mechanics Pavilion for the fight, and betting was heavy around the country. In the eighth round, Sharkey fell over in pain, claiming he had been hit by a low blow. Wyatt had not seen the punch clearly, but he believed Sharkey and declared him the winner. Loud boos rang out from the crowd, many of whom thought Sharkey was faking his injury. Newspapers the next day attacked Wyatt for his decision. There was even a demeaning editorial cartoon in the *New York Herald* that showed Wyatt as a Wild West outlaw, brandishing a revolver and holding a bag containing a $10,000 bribe. The cartoon's caption read: "The Bad Man Referee."

Wyatt's friend and fellow lawman Bill Tilghman (left) became famous for clearing outlaws from Oklahoma Territory during the 1890s.

The bad publicity from the fight brought Wyatt's name back into headlines. Suddenly articles began appearing everywhere, most of them critical. It seemed as though every enemy Wyatt had made during his years in the Wild West was talking to reporters and trying to get back at him. Wyatt and Josie packed up their belongings and headed far away—this time to the Yukon, where gold had been discovered. They opened a successful bar in Nome, Alaska, and managed to save $80,000 over the next few years.

When gold was found in Nevada in 1901, the Earps headed there, too. Once again, they failed to strike it rich, and poor investments ate up most of their savings. So it was back to California, this time to Los Angeles, where Wyatt would live out the last 20 years of his life. Now in his 60s, Wyatt found work helping the Los Angeles police chase down some bandits in Mexico. Later, he served as an adviser in Hollywood, suggesting authentic touches to add to silent movies about the Old West. Wyatt became close friends with western stars Tom Mix and William S. Hart and even considered being in the movies himself.

Early in 1928, as Wyatt was nearing his 80th birthday, he became greatly concerned that his side of the events that had happened in Kansas and Arizona would never be told. So he began sharing his old stories with a magazine writer named Stuart Lake, who specialized in features about the Old West. The two men met several times, and the tales that Lake heard thrilled him. He began a three-year process of research and writing. Before Lake could complete his book, however, Wyatt contracted the flu and died quietly at home on January 13, 1929.

Two years later, Lake's book, *Wyatt Earp: Frontier Marshal*, hit bookstores and became an instant bestseller. Lake had taken Wyatt's stories and embellished them with his own touches, turning Wyatt into a Western "Superman." In the book, Lake had Wyatt tell most of the stories, though many of the words were probably the author's. How much of the book was fact, and how much of it was fiction? No one was really sure. But one thing was clear— Stuart Lake had helped Americans find a new hero.

Lightning Fast and Deadly

I n stories, movies, and television broadcasts, Wyatt Earp is portrayed as a man who often faces down outlaws. He outdraws them with lightning speed and then shoots them dead. The reality was very different. Wyatt most often used his gun to "buffalo" lawbreakers rather than shoot them; he claimed that he killed only one man during his years in Dodge City. That is why it is ironic that Wyatt is most often remembered for the deadly shootout in Tombstone and the killings committed during his "vendetta ride." Wyatt is said also to have explained that being able to draw quickly was not always the best way to win a gunfight. It was better to draw deliberately and make sure you hit your target. According to Stuart Lake, in the Gunfight at the O.K. Corral, the cowboys shot 17 times with only 3 bullets hitting their targets, while the lawmen connected on 13 of their 17 shots.

CHAPTER FOUR

Long May His Story Be Told

THERE IS A FAMOUS EXPRESSION ABOUT BUSINESS THAT GOES,

"TIMING IS EVERYTHING."

When Stuart Lake's book about Wyatt Earp was published in 1931,

the United States was immersed in the

Great Depression and was also

DEALING WITH PROHIBITION.

In large American cities such as Chicago and New York, dangerous gangsters were constantly in the news, and crime seemed to be at its high point. What Americans needed was a brave, incorruptible lawman who could stand up to the bad guys and clean up the streets. What they needed was someone like Wyatt Earp—particularly the heroic figure portrayed in the pages of *Wyatt Earp: Frontier Marshal*.

Burt Lancaster (left) and Kirk Douglas (right) played Wyatt Earp and Doc Holliday in the 1957 movie Gunfight at the O.K. Corral.

Soon after the book appeared, Western scholars began to take it apart. Wyatt Earp had never been more than a deputy marshal any place he served, they noted, so the title *Frontier Marshal* was an exaggeration. A 17-year-old boy would probably not have been entrusted with driving a stagecoach in California, they claimed. The "Buntline special" with the extra-long barrel that Lake said Wyatt used might not have been real. Some of the exploits Lake credited to Wyatt may have really been those of Bat Masterson, Bill Tilghman, or other Western lawmen. But readers didn't care if all of the incidents in Lake's book had happened exactly the way he described them. They were too wrapped up in the adventure.

Scholars and historians continue to wonder about the tales that Lake spun in his book and to debate just what happened before, during, and after the shootout in Tombstone. Were the actions of the Earps justified? Did they, in some way, instigate the showdown with the Clantons? What really happened during the vendetta ride? Was Wyatt Earp just as lawless as the men he hunted down?

A large number of carefully researched biographies and other studies have been added to libraries since 1931 to try to answer some of these questions. The writers of these books don't view Wyatt as heroically as Stuart Lake did, but they do see him as a man who almost always acted quickly and decisively, and who was unafraid to face danger head-on.

Moviegoers in the 1930s were also interested in stories in which wide-open Western towns were tamed by lawmen like Wyatt Earp. At the time, Hollywood studios were expanding and looking for

Stuart Lake

Writer Stuart Lake always had an interest in the Old West. His fascination grew even stronger when he worked on newspapers with Bat Masterson in the early 1900s and heard firsthand stories about Dodge City and Wyatt Earp. In the mid-1920s, Lake moved to California, hoping to track down Wyatt to interview him for a magazine article or a book. As it turned out, Wyatt was also looking to find a biographer at the same time. The two men met several times, with Wyatt providing Lake with the "barest facts" about his life. Lake brought these facts to life, adding a lot of his own touches. Wyatt was always modest and never saw himself as a hero, but Lake had other ideas. Lake's book, *Wyatt Earp: Frontier Marshal*, presented a larger-than-life version of Wyatt and inspired a string of stories, movies, and television programs about lawmen and outlaws in Dodge City and Tombstone. Lake retold the story of the Earps and Tombstone in 1946, when he wrote the book that John Ford developed into his classic movie *My Darling Clementine*.

ideas for movies that would attract big audiences. Westerns, popular during the silent era, were even more in demand as "talkies." Lake's book inspired several movies in the 1930s and even more in later years.

Some people consider the 1946 film *My Darling Clementine*, directed by John Ford, to be one of the finest westerns ever made. Wyatt and his brothers are the main characters in the movie, and the showdown between the Earps and the Clanton gang at the O.K. Corral is its central moment. The movie has many inaccuracies—for example, the shootout occurs after the Clantons have killed both Virgil and Jim Earp, and the gunfight is longer and far bloodier than the real event—but its drama and excitement still thrill audiences. A decade later (in 1957), moviegoers relived another exaggerated Hollywood version of the Tombstone shootout in *Gunfight at the O.K. Corral*. Both movies can still often be seen on late-night television.

Wyatt Earp was the focus of two popular movies in the 1990s, too—*Tombstone* (1993) and *Wyatt Earp* (1994). Both movies portray a more realistic Wyatt, complete with flaws. But, in both, Wyatt's courage and integrity come through clearly to another generation of Americans.

Wyatt may also have been a part of numerous other westerns in which he was not even a featured character. Hollywood's most famous western star, John Wayne, often told friends that he had met Wyatt when the actor first arrived in Hollywood. Wayne added that each of the lawmen he played had a little bit of Wyatt Earp in him.

Wyatt and Wyatt-based characters have been even more popular on television than in the movies. In the 1950s, the television show *The Life and Legend of Wyatt Earp* ranked high in the ratings. It featured a town sheriff who cleaned up Dodge City using a long-barreled "Buntline special." Unlike the real Wyatt, his television namesake often got into shootouts with bad guys and was famous for his lightning-fast draw. The show is probably best known for the chorus of its theme song:

> *Wyatt Earp, Wyatt Earp,*
> *Brave, courageous, and bold.*
> *Long live his fame and long live his glory,*
> *And long may his story be told.*

TV's longest-running western, *Gunsmoke*, also set in Dodge City during the time Wyatt Earp served there, starred a hardworking marshal named Matt Dillon, who had some of Wyatt's qualities. It also featured places like the Long Branch Saloon that Wyatt may have frequented. Reruns of *Gunsmoke* are still shown on TV almost every day.

Wyatt's name has come up in some other unusual contexts, too. Several years ago, when U.S. Marines arrived in the African country of Somalia to try to quell violence and civil war going on there, the Marine colonel announced, "This place may be Dodge City, but we're Wyatt Earp."

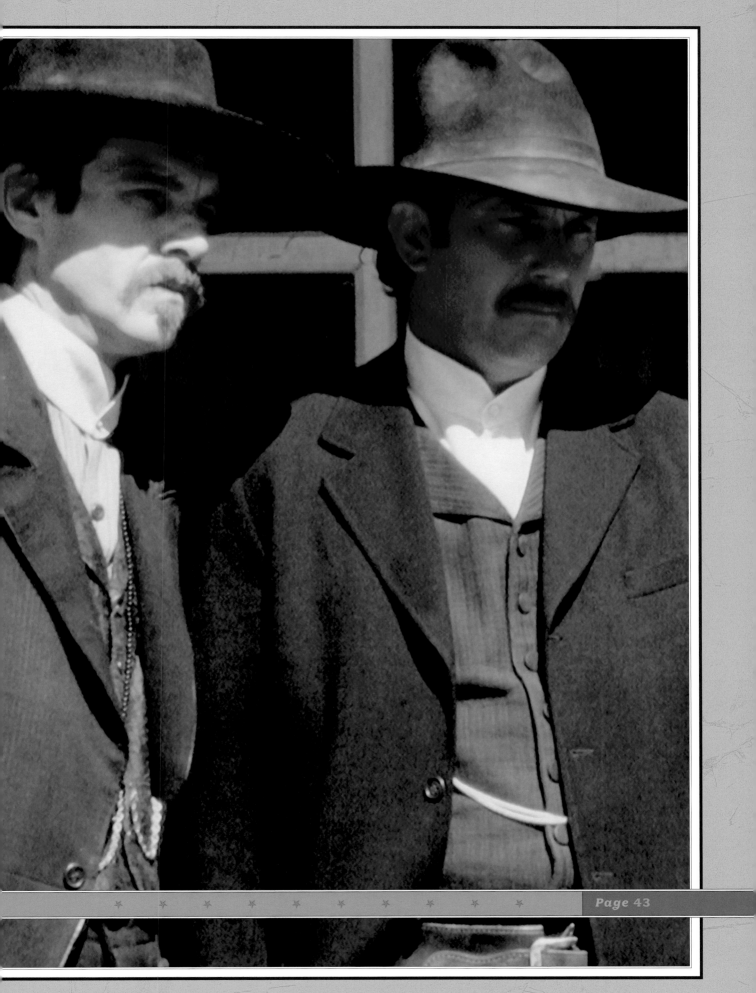

The 1994 movie Wyatt Earp starred Dennis Quaid (left) as Doc Holliday and Kevin Costner (right) as Wyatt Earp.

Wyatt's picture has appeared on several American postage stamps, and he even has a town named after him. Earp, California, located in the desert on the Arizona border, is not far from a group of mines that Wyatt once owned.

Bat Masterson once said, "The real story of the Old West will never be told unless Wyatt Earp will tell what he knows. . . ." Wyatt never really did tell his own story or reveal all of the secrets he knew about the Old West. Much of what is known about him is a mixture of praise from his friends and admirers and condemnation from his enemies and critics. But writers and filmmakers continue to enhance his legend, and historians keep searching for the real man inside.

Gunfight at the O.K. Corral

The shootout on the streets of Tombstone on October 26, 1881, is a true symbol of the Wild West. Contrary to many of the legends about the event, the gunfight did not actually take place inside the O.K. Corral. Its location was an open lot about a block away from the corral, between two boarding-houses and Fly's Photo Studio. How did it become wrongly named? A newspaper reporter probably thought that setting the shootout in a corral sounded more authentically Western. Several movies portraying the gunfight have also exaggerated how long it took. In reality, it was over in less than 30 seconds. The headline in the local paper the next morning read: "Three Men Hurled into Eternity in the Duration of a Moment." While the shootout was over quickly, the murder trial of the Earp brothers and Doc Holliday lasted several months. John Behan was the chief witness against the Earps, but his testimony was contradicted by several eyewitnesses. The charges were ulti-mately dismissed.

Further Information

BOOKS

Barra, Allen. *Inventing Wyatt Earp: His Life and Many Legends*. New York: Carroll & Graf Publishers, 1998.

Marks, Paula Mitchell. *And Die in the West—The Story of the O.K. Corral Gunfight*. New York: William Morrow & Co., 1989.

Tefertiller, Casey. *Wyatt Earp: The Life Behind the Legend*. New York: John Wiley & Sons, 1997.

FILMS

Gunfighters of the Old West. 1992. 90 min. Simitar Entertainment.

My Darling Clementine. 2003 (videocassette release of a 1946 motion picture). 96 min. Twentieth Century Fox Home Entertainment.

Wyatt Earp: Justice at the OK Corral. 1993. 50 min. A&E Home Video.

WEB SITES

Court TV's Crime Library—Wyatt Earp: Knight with a Six-Shooter
http://www.crimelibrary.com/gangsters_outlaws/outlaws/earp/1.html

People of the Old West
http://www.42explore2.com/oldwest2.htm

Tombstone History Page
http://www.tombstonehistory.com

Index